Comptroller of the Currency
Administrator of National Banks

I0439049

Sampling Methodologies

Comptroller's Handbook

August 1998

EP

Sampling Methodologies — Table of Contents

Background

It is usually impractical or impossible to review all items or files when examining an area of bank operations, especially if the volume of information is large. Examiners use sampling to observe a random subset to learn about the multitude of items from which they are drawn. Upon drawing statistical inferences from this subset, they can state with a certain level of confidence that the inferences apply to the population as a whole.

Benefits of using statistical sampling include:

- The ability to quantify results and relate them to the entire portfolio being reviewed.

- The ability to quantify sampling risk (i.e., the risk that the sample is not indicative of the entire portfolio).

- Effective use of limited examiner resources.

This booklet discusses statistical sampling in general, as well as specific methods of designing, selecting, and evaluating statistically valid samples.

The two types of statistical sampling methods discussed most prominently in this booklet are numerical sampling and proportional sampling. In numerical sampling, each item in a population is equally likely to be drawn. In proportional sampling, the likelihood of an item being selected is proportional to the item's size.

An examiner's choice of a sampling method depends on the specific objectives of the supervisory activity. Sometimes, examiners may choose a sampling method that is not statistical — that is, they may want to rely on judgment or specific knowledge about a population in selecting files for review. Examiners do not use the results from a judgmentally derived sample to draw conclusions about a larger population. Often, the specific knowledge or judgment used to derive the nonstatistical sample is used to develop statistically valid samples that divide the population into groups. Each group, or stratum, can then be reviewed, intensively if necessary. Such sampling improves the examination process.

This booklet provides guidance on which sampling methods are best for specific areas of examination interest. Although the discussion is geared toward sampling loan portfolios, other types of items — investments, deposits, and off-balance-sheet accounts — can be sampled. By sampling, examiners can test the effectiveness of processes, policies, controls, management information systems, or risk management practices.

OCC Policy

The OCC generally does not require the use of any specific sampling methodology. Unless specifically addressed in a handbook section or other policy guidance, the use of sampling in a supervisory activity, as well as the type of sampling used, is left to the discretion of the examiner-in-charge (EIC). The "Sampling Objectives" portion of this booklet addresses matters that examiners must consider in determining an appropriate sampling approach as part of a bank's supervisory strategy.

From time to time, OCC senior management may recommend a specific sampling method for examining certain on- or off-balance-sheet accounts. They may also provide guidance on which parameters to use in selecting a sample. Such guidance may be part of a year's OCC operating plan, as well as other OCC issuances. For example, the examination procedures for fair lending and community bank consumer compliance have specific guidance on sampling methods.

When conducting statistical sampling, examiners should use the following guidelines:

- The populations to be sampled should be the portfolios identified in the bank's approved supervisory strategy. If the focus is on the internally rated nonclassified portion of the bank's loan portfolio, the population should generally exclude Shared National Credit (SNC) loans. However, there may be circumstances (e.g., testing for process, policy or underwriting exceptions) in which examiners are justified in including SNC loans in the sample population. The population should also exclude "credit basket" loans (small business loans requiring limited documentation as outlined in the March 30, 1993 "Interagency Policy Statement on Documentation of Loans").

  - If the bank's management information system accurately reports legally binding commitments, the sample should be selected on the commitment amount. When the sample can be selected by either the note (an individual loan) or the borrower, examiners should choose the borrower.

- The sampling plans for banks that are part of multibank holding companies should be consistent for all national banks in the company. For example, if the company strategy calls for using proportional sampling when reviewing the quality of commercial loans in one of the five national bank subsidiaries, the EIC should use proportional sampling on the commercial loans at each of the other subsidiary banks.

- The EIC should deem statistical sampling reasonable and feasible with respect to the national bank being examined. The size and composition of the sample should be commensurate with the risk characteristics of the population being tested. Common sense and judgment are critical in determining the focus and extent of testing. The examiner should consider any known resource constraints on the bank or examining personnel relating to time, personnel, and costs. These include, but are not limited to, actual or projected sample sizes, availability of examining and bank staff, availability of data processing hardware and software, and any other pertinent factors.

- Although proportional and numerical sampling can be done manually, an automated sampling program or module can be more efficient and less burdensome. Examiners should try to use a bank's own automated sampling program, if available. Examiners may also use other available automated programs.

- Because precision and reliability levels (i.e., statistical assurance) affect the size of samples, the OCC recommends that examiners use the following guidelines. For proportional sampling, examiners should use precision levels of 5 percent, 10 percent, 15 percent, or 20 percent and reliability levels of 80 percent, 86 percent, 90 percent, or 95 percent. For numerical sampling, examiners should use precision levels of 5 percent or 10 percent and reliability levels of 90 percent or 95 percent. This booklet discusses statistical assurance in a later section.

Sampling Objectives

Supervisory strategies for national banks should specifically note if the examination process will use sampling. Based upon the objectives of the supervisory activities, the strategy should identify the portfolios to sample, the type of sampling to use, and the purpose of the sampling. If examination planning activities indicate a previously unidentified need for sampling, the EIC should change the strategy to note this.

In determining the type of sampling to use, examiners consider the quantity, quality, and nature of the population to be reviewed; the bank's risk management systems; the bank's appetite for risk; the objectives and benefits of the different sampling methods; the purpose and objective of the sample; and resource constraints. Examiners may choose which of the three sampling methods — judgmental, proportional, or numerical — will best meet the objectives of supervisory strategy.

The following list highlights some strategic objectives that examiners may want to meet by using sampling.

- Commercial loans, commercial real estate loans, floor plan, and receivable financing:

  - Validate risk management and internal problem loan identification systems or test process effectiveness.

  - Identify additional credit risk exposure in the sampled portfolio.

  - Determine compliance with underwriting standards.

  - Identify administrative weaknesses (e.g., financial statement or other documentation exceptions).

  - Assess the adequacy of the allowance for loan and lease losses (ALLL).

- Retail loans (e.g., consumer paper, credit card, check credit, residential real estate, and home equity lending):

  - Validate adherence to appropriate performance reporting standards by checking extension or re-aging history.

  - Determine lien perfection status.

  - Assess compliance with underwriting standards through a review of overrides, extensions, renewals or other loans.

  - Determine compliance with laws and regulations (e.g., consumer compliance).

- Municipal investments or derivatives:

  - Validate risk management systems.

  - Identify credit or market risk exposure.

  - Determine compliance with investment standards.

  - Identify administrative weaknesses (e.g., financial statement or other documentation exceptions).

- Deposit accounts:

  - Verify the accuracy of the interest rate, terms, and conditions when compared to the disclosed contractual information.

  - Determine compliance with a bank's deposit policies.

  - Identify weaknesses in a bank's deposit operations.

  - Determine compliance with applicable laws and regulations.

- Consumer compliance:

  - Determine compliance with fair lending laws and regulations.

  - Determine compliance with truth-in-lending and other consumer compliance disclosure requirements.

  - Evaluate the reliability of a bank's compliance management system.

Sampling Methods

Nonstatistical Sampling – Judgmental

Judgmental sampling is sampling without statistical measurement. The OCC has historically used, and continues to use, nonstatistical judgmental sampling in its examinations. Using sound judgment and knowledge of a bank's policies, controls, and systems, examiners identify the bank's areas of greatest risk exposure and select items for review.

Judgmental sampling allows examiners to review an identified percentage (coverage) of a specific population. Although examiners cannot statistically relate the results of this sample to the entire population of items, they can identify specific exceptions. The results of the judgmental sample are considered when examiners evaluate the quality of the population reviewed. Examiners should comment on exceptions, identifying the root causes of those exceptions. For example, exceptions noted in a review of loan documentation on instalment loan extensions could be the result of bank personnel's lack of training or inadequate knowledge of bank policy.

Statistical Sampling – Proportional

Proportional sampling is appropriate when the dollar amount of items is relevant to the objective of a procedure, particularly when those dollar amounts vary significantly. In proportional sampling, the population to be sampled is defined by dollar amount. Large dollar amounts have a greater chance of being selected than smaller ones; all items greater than a certain amount and a representative number of smaller items are selected. Proportional sampling is useful to examiners evaluating the quality of a loan portfolio because of the effect larger dollar items can have on asset quality. Sometimes, a strategic objective will call specifically for this approach.

The objective of the sample is to review items for a specific characteristic, which is also called the feature of interest. The OCC has historically endorsed the use of proportional sampling to discover additional classified loans in commercial loan portfolios. Proportional sampling also is appropriate when examiners want to test population items for monetary errors (i.e., incorrect finance charges, incorrect late charges) or compliance errors (i.e., compliance with underwriting standards, incomplete disclosure statements).

Statistical Sampling – Numerical

In numerical sampling, the population to be sample is defined by the number of items. Numerical sampling is usually used to reveal the presence (or absence) of a defined characteristic in a portfolio of items with similar characteristics. Each item in the population has the same probability of selection as any other. Therefore, examiners may evaluate the results of applying numerical sampling and the related examination of selected items only in terms of the number of errors or exceptions. This statistical sampling method is appropriate for examination procedures in which the frequency of errors, exceptions, or another feature of interest is of primary concern and the dollar amount of the exception is not considered relevant.

This method is a valid sampling procedure for determining adherence to a requirement, such as a bank's underwriting standards or interagency classification policies for delinquent loans. The OCC has historically endorsed the use of numerical sampling to evaluate retail credit portfolios such as instalment loans and residential real estate loans. Examiners can use numerical sampling to gain a broad perspective about the adequacy of a bank's administrative controls and practices. Sample results can indicate the effectiveness of these systems but do not provide a quantitative measure of the results. Depending upon the sample objectives, results are indicated by the level of compliance with a bank's administrative controls, banking laws and regulations, bank policy, or OCC policy.

Application of Methods of Sampling

Following are suggestions for applying statistical sampling plans and specific procedures to areas of examination interest:

Program	Examples of Sampling Procedures
Due From Banks	Use proportional sampling to select accounts whose reconcilements are to be reviewed.
Investment Securities	Use proportional sampling to select municipal securities and money market holdings to determine compliance with investment standards.
Bank Dealer Activities	Use proportional sampling to select trading account securities for examination.
Loan Portfolio Management	Use proportional or numerical sampling to validate internal loan review.
Commercial Loans Accounts Receivable Floor Plan Commercial Real Estate Commercial Lease Financing Indirect Dealer Lines	Use proportional or numerical sampling to evaluate credit quality, compliance with underwriting standards, accuracy of internal risk rating.
Instalment Loans Credit Cards Check Credit Home Equity Residential Real Estate	Use numerical sampling to test: – The accuracy of MIS, such as bank-prepared past due, problem loan listing, and insider loans. – Renewals, deferrals and extensions for compliance with policy, degree of usage, accuracy of reporting. – Score overrides for compliance with policy guidelines and fair lending laws and regulations, documentation, reasonableness of credit decision. – Recently extended loans for compliance with underwriting policy, credit criteria, laws and regulations.
Other Real Estate Owned	Use proportional sampling to test for policy adherence, when appropriate, based on number and volume.
Deposit Accounts	Use numerical sampling to select accounts to test computation of interest, early withdrawal penalty, compliance with laws and regulations.

Fiduciary Accounts	Use numerical sampling to test compliance with trust agreements.
Off-balance-sheet accounts	Depending upon the sample objectives, use either proportional or numerical sampling.
Consumer Compliance	Use numerical sampling to identify a sample for Truth-in-Lending or Truth-in-Savings reviews, or to test the integrity of HMDA and CRA small business lending reports.
Community Reinvestment Act	Use numerical sampling to select sample for comparison of credit extended inside and outside a bank's assessment area or to perform a lending test.

Examples of how to sample for specific objectives:

Objective	Suggested Method
Identify unrecognized classified loans in commercial loan portfolios.	Proportional sample of all loans that are not internally rated.
Validate current internal risk ratings and identify classified loans in commercial loan portfolios.	Proportional or numerical sample of all commercial loans, both those that are internally rated and those that are not.
Test for compliance with underwriting practices and, credit criteria, documentation, pricing and terms.	Numerical or proportional sample from new assets booked since the last policy, e.g., examination for a defined period (e.g., 30 to 90 days).
Test for compliance of credit score loan overrides with policy and fair lending laws and regulations by checking compliance with guidelines, documentation of reason for override, and appropriateness of credit decision.	Numerical sample of new loans that scored below a cutoff, but were approved in the recent past (e.g., 30 to 90 days).

Test loan renewals and extensions for compliance with policy, degree of usage, and accuracy of reporting.	Numerical sample from the entire population to test usage and accuracy of reporting, or numerical sample from the bank's renewal and extension listing to test for compliance with policy.
Determine accuracy of the bank's management information system.	Numerical sample from the entire population and trace reportable items to appropriate listings, e.g., past due, renewals and extensions, re-agings, prepayments, and insider loans.
Identify risk exposure in the municipal bond Portfolio.	Proportional sample of all municipal bonds and evaluate the sample for asset quality.
Determine accuracy of the bank's external reports, such as HMDA and CRA small business reports.	Numerical sample from the entire population to test the accuracy of reported data.
Determine compliance of deposit accounts with policy guidelines, deposit contract terms, and applicable laws and regulations.	Numerical sample of deposit accounts booked within the last six months or since the last examination and determine compliance with bank policy. Ensure that rates and terms of the deposit are in agreement with the contract and any applicable laws and regulations.
Determine compliance of fiduciary accounts with trust agreements.	Numerical sample of all accounts or accounts booked since the last examination and evaluate the accounts to ensure that the accounts are being handled in accordance with the trust agreement.

Statistical Sampling Assurance

Precision

"Precision" is the examiner's tolerance for exceptions in the sample. Normally, precision implies a range of acceptable values. Most examination procedures are designed to test exceptions to a bank's risk management systems, i.e., its policies, practices, and procedures. Since few exceptions should exist, sampling procedures are concerned primarily with the upper precision limit. Examiners want to know the greatest effect (the upper precision) that sampling exceptions will have on the bank's condition. They should adequately document in working papers their reasons for selecting a certain precision value. Examiners should consider quantity of risk, direction of risk, and quality of risk management in determining precision levels to use. In designing samples, the precision limit affects the sample size; the smaller the precision limits, the larger the size of the sample selected.

Proportional Sampling

When examiners use proportional sampling, precision is set using a percentage of Tier 1 capital plus the allowance for loan and lease losses (ALLL). The larger the quantity or number of exceptions the EIC can tolerate, the larger the precision limit should be. Examiners should base the precision limit for proportional samples on their knowledge of a bank's financial and operating conditions.

Examiners should consider:

- The composition of the bank's portfolio. For example, the examiner may tolerate more exceptions in a loan portfolio segment supported by liquid or marketable collateral than in one secured by real estate construction loans.

- The bank's risk management systems and controls. The better the bank's risk management system, the more exceptions an examiner may tolerate (in the belief that the bank will identify deficiencies).

- The amount of previously identified classified loans. If a bank has a high level of classified loans, the examiner may select a lower precision level because she or he is less tolerant of additional classified loans in the portfolio.

- The local economy. If the local economy is strong and stable, the examiner may tolerate more exceptions than if the economy is experiencing a decline.

Individual bank circumstances may support a precision limit of 5 percent, 10 percent, 15 percent, or a maximum of 20 percent for proportional sampling. (Any value less than 20 percent can be chosen; for discussion purposes in this booklet, increments of five are used.) When an examiner can tolerate few exceptions, a precision of 5 percent is normally chosen. When an examiner can tolerate a large rate of exceptions, a precision of 20 percent is normally chosen. Precision levels greater than 20 percent are not recommended.

For example, assume that since its last examination, a bank began extending a significant amount of new loans to the cable television industry. The bank's loan review division has not performed an in-depth review of this area before the scheduled examination date. Several of these credits appear on the delinquency report. Based on reported delinquencies in a portfolio not yet internally reviewed, the examiner may select a precision of 5 percent and the sample size will be relatively large.

On the other hand, when a bank's internal classified figure is low, it is sufficiently capitalized, the examiner has confidence in the internal loan review system, sound control systems are in place, and the nonclassified commercial loan portfolio is to be reviewed, a precision of 20 percent and a relatively small sample may be appropriate.

Numerical Sampling

An examiner sets a precision limit in numerical sampling by deciding how many exception items can be tolerated in the sample population. The more exceptions the examiner can tolerate, the higher the precision limit should be. Because noncompliance indicates weakness in policies, systems, or controls, bankers and examiners should have a low tolerance for exceptions in that area. Examiners should consider setting the precision level at 5 percent or 10 percent.

Reliability

"Reliability" is the level of confidence in sample results. Selecting a reliability level will affect the size of a sample: the higher the reliability level, the greater the number of items examiners will review. Examiners should document in working papers why they selected a certain reliability level. They should not select reliability levels without considering the bank's financial condition, risk profile and risk management systems. The more confidence examiners have in the institution and its risk management process, the fewer OCC examiner resources should be needed to evaluate transactions.

Reliability factors are numbers that reflect reliability levels (95 percent reliability equates to a 3.0 factor; 80 percent reliability equals a 1.6 factor). Reliability factors are used to determine sample sizes and precision adjustment factors. When exceptions are found, examiners use reliability factors to adjust previously selected precision limits to evaluate sample results and perform statistical sampling projections. (See examples in this booklet's section "Sampling Plans" under "Sample Design and Selection" and "Numerical Sample Evaluation Worksheet Example.") The reliability factors in this booklet, which are taken from Poisson probability distributions (see glossary for definition), are approximations of the probability of finding at least one exception in a sample of selected items at a given reliability level and error rate. Reliability factors and their associated reliability levels and precision adjustment factors are noted in appendixes C and D and are common references for audit sampling purposes.

Examiners should consider four different reliability levels when using proportional statistical sampling – 95 percent, 90 percent, 86 percent, and 80 percent. These levels allow examiners some flexibility in structuring the sample based on an assessment of the factors mentioned at the beginning of this section and the resultant tolerance for exceptions. These levels also allow examiners to control the associated degree of sampling risk (defined below).

Two reliability levels should normally be considered for numerical sampling — 90 percent and 95 percent. Because the objective of numerical sampling is generally to determine whether the bank adheres to a policy, system, or control, the OCC desires a high degree of confidence (i.e., minimal sampling risk) in the results.

Sampling Risk

Sampling risk is the difference of one minus the reliability level. With 95 percent reliability, the sampling risk is 5 percent. This means that 5 percent of the time the results of the sample may not be truly indicative of the entire portfolio. With 80 percent reliability, the sampling risk is 20 percent. This means that 20 percent of the time, or one time in five, the results of the sample may not be truly indicative of the entire portfolio. Because the objective of sampling is to test for deviations from a bank's policies, procedures or practices, the OCC wants to maintain sampling risk at levels that allow a high degree of confidence in sample results and their validity. Sampling risk greater than 20 percent is not acceptable.

Sampling Plans

When sampling is used, examiners devise a sample plan to make the most efficient and effective use of resources to meet the objectives of the review. Each sample plan design involves the same concepts:

- Population selection.
- Sample design and sample selection.
- Sample evaluation and interpretation of results.

The following comments and examples are provided to illustrate the sampling plan design process for the three sampling methodologies. Although the comments and examples below relate to the commercial and instalment loan portfolios, examiners can use sampling in any asset, liability, or off-balance-sheet account.

Population Selection

In population selection, examiners decide which portfolios to sample. They do so by considering the approved strategy for the bank and the objectives of the examination. Strategies may call for examiners to review the entire commercial loan portfolio or focus on particular types of loans. Types are grouped by credit, industry affiliation, or bank lending division. Selecting a very broad category, such as the entire commercial loan portfolio, can result in a very large sample size. When possible, examiners should consider further segmenting such large portfolios to reduce the workload. To make statistically valid conclusions, examiners must define or stratify (group) the selected population as much as possible by their characteristics.

For OCC purposes, assets generally can be grouped into two categories. In one category are assets that typically use common, uniform underwriting standards (e.g., one-to-four-family residential real estate loans, consumer instalment loans, credit card loans, home improvement loans, home equity loans, and overdraft lines of credit). In the other category are assets with broader common characteristics, such as type of credit, industry, or bank division (e.g., commercial real estate loans, real estate construction or development loans, municipal investment securities, private placements, oil and gas loans, and mortgage warehousing).

Example of Population Selection — Judgmental Sampling

The examiner is concerned about the accuracy of the bank's risk grading system for commercial real estate loans identified as problem credits. In judgmental sampling, an examiner may decide to review files for commercial real estate loans of $500,000 or more that are internally classified. The examiner reviews all files selected.

Example of Population Selection — Proportional Sampling

The examiner wants to determine whether the nonclassified loans in a bank's asset-based lending division pose unrecognized risk. Proportional sampling can be used effectively to select a statistical sample of loans internally rated pass. This portfolio is considered "grouped" because the population includes all nonclassified loans in this particular division.

Example of Population Selection — Numerical Sampling

The examiner is concerned about the number of overrides in a bank's instalment loan portfolio. The examiner can use numerical sampling to test the extent of compliance with the bank's override policy.

Sample Design and Selection

In sample design and selection, the examiner determines which items should be in the sample and bases selection of the sample items on selected reliability and precision levels. Examiners can conduct a statistical sample manually or by using an automated sampling program.

Sample Selection — Judgmental Sampling

The examiner uses sound judgment to determine and select items for review. For example, the selected loans might include ten loans extended since the last examination, five significant doubtful-rated classified loans, seven large-dollar substandard loans, two new loans to insiders, and any other type of loan that the examiner decides to review. The examiner determines whether the internal loan rating is accurate (by reviewing the loans' quality) and whether the underwriting standards are safe and sound.

Sample Selection — Proportional Sampling

Sample design, with a proportional statistical sample, consists of selecting the reliability and precision.

To select sample items from loan portfolios, the examiner may use the same criteria followed by the bank's internal loan review. Alternatively, the examiner can sample from every loan in the population or, to eliminate a loan review of small dollar loans, the examiner can specify that the sample is taken of all loans exceeding a certain dollar amount.

When examining the internally rated, nonclassified commercial loan portfolio, loans to be excluded from the sample are ones extended as part of the minimal loan documentation program, i.e., "credit basket" loans. Additionally, shared national credits might be excluded from samples designed to test risk rating accuracy because they are reviewed separately as part of a specific program.

With the internally rated, nonclassified commercial loan portfolio, examiners might consider using a precision level of 20 percent and a reliability level of 80 percent. These levels can be justified when the bank has adequate capital, acceptable internal loan review, sound risk management systems, and good asset quality.

Once examiners establish precision and reliability, the sample is selected. The size for a proportional sample (based on selecting the sample by note) is estimated as:

$$\frac{\text{population amount in \$}}{\text{monetary interval}} = \text{sample size (\# of items)}$$

The monetary interval is calculated as:

$$\frac{(\text{Tier 1 capital} + \text{ALLL}) \times \text{precision level as a decimal}}{\text{reliability factor (From table 1, appendix C)}}$$

NOTE: (Tier 1 capital + ALLL) x precision level is also known as monetary precision.

Stated another way, the equation for estimating the sample size is as follows:

$$\text{population amount in \$} \quad \times \quad \frac{\text{reliability factor}}{\text{monetary precision}} \quad = \quad \text{sample size}$$

Examples of calculations: An examiner is examining a regional bank with $345 million in Tier 1 capital plus the ALLL. The nonclassified commercial loan portfolio, excluding "basket" and, if warranted, SNC loans, is $1.3 billion.

1. With a desired precision level of 20 percent and a reliability level of 80 percent, the equation for calculating the monetary interval is:

$$\frac{\$345\text{MM} \times .20}{1.6} = \frac{\$69\text{MM}}{1.6} = \$43\text{MM}$$

The estimated sample size is equal to the dollar amount of the sample population divided by the monetary interval. (If the result is a fraction, the rule of thumb is to round down to the next whole number.)

$$\frac{\$1,300\text{MM}}{\$43\text{MM}} = 30 \text{ loans}$$

2. If the desired precision level is 5 percent and the reliability level is 95 percent, the equation for the monetary interval is:

$$\frac{\$345MM \times .05}{3} = \frac{\$17.25MM}{3} = \$5.75MM$$

The estimated sample size is equal to the sample population divided by the monetary interval.

$$\frac{\$1,300MM}{\$5.75MM} = 226 \text{ loans}$$

Once the appropriate sample design is completed, sample items need to be selected. The examiner must begin the sample selection from a random starting point. This starting point is a randomly chosen number between zero and the monetary interval.

For example, if the monetary interval is $5,750,000, the random numerical starting point must be a number between zero and 5,750,000. The random number may be obtained from various methods, such as a table of random numbers or the serial number of a dollar bill. Automated sampling software will normally have a random number generator feature.

Discussed below are two sample methods for selecting items using a standard calculator and the bank's trial balance or other report listing sample population items. For illustration, the following examples use 462,021 as the sample's random numerical start.

Cumulative total. Beginning with the first item on the trial balance, this method involves adding the dollar amount of each item to an ongoing total. The item whose balance results in the subtotal equaling or surpassing the random numerical start (e.g., $462,021) is chosen as the first sample item. The remaining sample items are selected by continually adding item amounts from the trial balance and selecting each item whose balance causes the subtotal to equal or exceed each increment of the monetary interval (i.e., $6,212,021, $11,962,021, etc.).

Negative/Positive. Beginning with the random numerical start entered into an adding machine as a negative number (e.g., -462,021), the dollar amounts of the trial balance items are added until they subtotal zero or a positive number. The item that triggers this event is selected as the first sample item. From the subtotal, the random numerical start is then continually subtracted until the subtotal again results in a negative number. Then the dollar amounts of the remaining trial balance items are added until the subtotal is again zero or a positive number. The item that triggers the zero or positive subtotal is the next sample item selection. This process is repeated to select each subsequent sample item until the population of items is exhausted.

Sample Selection — Numerical Sampling

The sample size for a numerical sample is determined by the reliability and precision levels selected.

$$\text{sample size} = \frac{\text{reliability factor (from table 1)}}{\text{precision (as a decimal)}}$$

The following chart shows the sample sizes associated with OCC desired precision and reliability levels for numerical sampling.

Sample Sizes

	Reliability - 90%	Reliability - 95%
Precision 5%	46	60
Precision 10%	23	30

When reliability is 95 percent (the corresponding reliability factor is 3.0, from appendixes C and D) and precision is 5 percent, the examiner selects 60 items.

When reliability is 90 percent (the corresponding reliability factor is 2.3, from appendixes C and D) and precision is 10 percent, the examiner selects 23 items. Although a sample of fewer than 30 items can be selected and reviewed, examiners should not project sample results based on such a small sample because of the high degree of error inherent in such a small sample population.

Examiners should use a bank's automated sampling software, if available, to perform numerical sampling. However, a numerical sample can be selected manually.

When selecting a numerical sample manually, examiners should divide the population size by the sample size to determine the sampling interval.

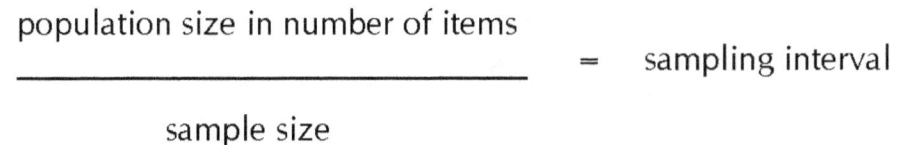

$$\frac{\text{population size in number of items}}{\text{sample size}} = \text{sampling interval}$$

(If the result is a fraction, the rule of thumb is to round down to the next whole number.)

For example, if there are a total of 1,000 override instalment loans, the sampling interval is 33 when reliability is 95 percent and precision is 10 percent (30-item sample size).

$$\frac{1,000}{30} = 33$$

The item that coincides with the random starting point (using a random number selected from a dollar bill, random number table, or other source) is the first sample item selected for review. The examiner continues counting and selecting subsequent items that coincide with the sampling interval.

The sampling interval for numerical sampling can also be derived using other selection techniques. These techniques include measured interval, specific position, and terminal digit, and are applied after determining the random starting point.

- Measured interval uses a set distance (e.g., inches) to select items for review. Each subsequent sample item will be the same measured interval from the last sample item. If the distance from the first sampled item on a trial balance to the second is five inches, the examiner measures every five inches on the trial balance and selects a sample item.

- Specific position uses a set position on each page of a list to select items for review. If, for example, the first selected sampled item was the last item on a page, the examiner could select that same item from each subsequent page.

- Terminal digit selects sample items using the same terminal digits, i.e., the one or more digits furthest to the right. Those items having the same terminal digits – for example, 0089, 0189, 0289 . . . 9989 – would be selected.

Sample Evaluation and Interpretation

In sample evaluation and interpretation, examiners review the sample results and draw conclusions about the entire population of data. By designing a sample plan, examiners attempt to control the risk of a significant deteriorating condition remaining undetected. The evaluation of the sample helps examiners achieve that objective.

Statisticians recommend that a sample be at least 30 items. When smaller samples are used to make projections about the population from which they are drawn, the degree of error is too great. Examiners can still pull samples of less than 30 items, but they should not be used to make projections about the larger population.

Judgmental Sampling

Sample results from nonstatistical sampling cannot be projected beyond the loans sampled. However, exceptions discovered when evaluating these credits may suggest a larger problem. The results of a judgmental sample are considered when examiners evaluate the quality of the population from which the sample was selected. Examiners should comment on exceptions and identify the nature and possible root causes of the exceptions. For example, an individual bank employee's lack of training or inadequate knowledge of bank policy could cause exceptions. Examiners should discuss exceptions and root causes with bank management.

Proportional Sampling

One of the OCC's objectives in performing a proportional statistical sample in a commercial loan portfolio is to identify exceptions. An exception in this case is, for example, a loan classified by the OCC but not classified by the bank. Such exceptions can either be full exceptions (the entire loan amount is classified) or partial exceptions (only a portion of the loan is classified).

When reviewing a sample of loans a bank has not classified, an examiner might consider screening loans using credit file information. Doing so could reduce file review time. Since none of the loans in the sample has been classified by the bank, only a minimal file review might be warranted. However, screening requires experience and knowledge (see the "Classification of Credit" section of the Comptroller's Handbook). When screening loans, examiners could answer the following questions:

- Is the purpose of the loan identified?

- Is the source of repayment identified and is the loan paying as agreed?

- Is the loan secured by marketable or liquid collateral?

- Is the financial statement current and does it support the source of repayment?

- Does the nature of the business warrant further consideration?

Based on the answers to these questions, examiners decide whether additional loan file analysis is necessary. If screening suggests that the loan should be classified, examiners must analyze it more extensively using traditional methods.

In this example of reviewing pass loans for rating accuracy, OCC examiners assign loan ratings (pass, special mention, substandard, doubtful, loss) to all sample loans reviewed. The degree of classification (substandard, doubtful, or loss) is not factored into a statistical probability evaluation; the significant factor is that the OCC considers the loan to be classified and the bank's internal loan review system has not classified it. If the OCC classifies a loan that the bank does not, the difference is an "exception of overstatement."

When an examiner reviews a portfolio containing both classified and nonclassified loans, the evaluation is conducted in a slightly different manner. Even if ratings are somewhat different (i.e., the OCC classifies the loan substandard, while internal loan review rates it doubtful), no exception exists for statistical sampling purposes. But an exception could exist if sampling was done on a population of loans all of which are rated substandard by the bank and a portion of which are rated doubtful by the OCC. If internal loan review rates a loan as classified and the OCC considers it a pass or special mention loan, the difference is an "exception of understatement."

Both understatements and overstatements are considered when interpreting sample results.

If no exceptions are found, the desired statistical assurance (reliability level and precision level) has been attained and no further evaluation is required. When exceptions are found, examiners should further analyze and evaluate the exceptions. Examiners should attempt to determine the root causes of exceptions and whether exceptions are isolated occurrences or a pattern or practice. Some possibilities to explain an exception could be:

- The inexperience of a bank officer.

- An intentional disregard for policies and procedures.

- Exception items unique to a particular type of asset, division in the bank, or industry.

- Internal reviewers assigning ratings differently because they misunderstood internal classification definitions.

- Untimeliness of bank rating changes (information was not available at the time of the internal review).

Examiners could identify other reasons for the exception. A reasonable explanation for an exception does not mean examiners should exclude it from sample results. Examiners should note causes of exceptions and discuss them with bank management. Examiners may recommend that management conduct its own review of exceptions.

If exceptions are found, the original reliability and precision levels are no longer valid. Examiners must revise their statistical assurance based upon sample findings, but should not enlarge the statistical sample or alter the reliability level. Enlarging the sample would assume that original sample exceptions were not representative of exceptions in the population and corrupt the statistical validity of the sample. However, the type and causes of exceptions noted may indicate a need for further testing under supervision by risk.

Since the reliability level is the confidence in the sample, changing reliability is not desirable. Therefore, examiners must adjust the precision level after identifying exceptions. Appendixes C and D are tables that examiners can use to arrive at precision-adjusted exception levels. Appendix C determines the adjusted precision for overstatement exceptions; appendix D determines the adjusted precision for understatement exceptions.

A proportional sample evaluation worksheet will help examiners evaluate the sample (see examples of completed worksheets on the following two pages). By projecting the value of all sample exceptions to the population from which the sample was selected, the worksheets arrive at an estimated additional percentage of classified loans in the commercial loan portfolio.

The worksheet can be prepared manually or in an automated format. Instructions for the worksheet can be found in appendix A.

PROPORTIONAL SAMPLE EVALUATION WORKSHEET I

Example: A statistical sample was conducted of all commercial loans rated "pass" by the bank's Internal Loan Review (ILR). ILR identified a total of $362,413,000 classified commercial loans (105 percent of Tier 1 + ALLL). A review of the sample items resulted in four loans (all below the cutoff, i.e., the monetary interval) being classified by the examiner which the bank considered Pass. This example worksheet is completed to show how the value of those exceptions relate to the precision factor.

Tier 1 Capital + ALLL: $ 345MM   Reliability: 90 %   Precision: 10 %   Monetary Precision(MP) $ 34.5MM   Monetary Interval (MI): $ 15MM

OCC Rating	Borrower	Loan Balance (L)	Sample Exception (SE)	Sample Interval MI/L = SI	Cutoff Loans	Population Exception SE x SI = PE	Rank	Precision Adjustment Factor (P)	Precision-adjusted Exception PE x P
		$2,188	$2,188	6.8556		$15,000	1	1.59	$23,850
		$6,007	$2,857	2.4971		$ 7,134	3	1.36	$ 9,702
		$3,850	$3,850	3.8961		$15,000	2	1.44	$21,600
		$ 200	$ 40	75.0000		$ 3,000	4	1.32	$ 3,960
	TOTALS		$8,935			$40,134			$59,112

RESULTS:

Precision-adjusted Exceptions = $ 59,112

Precision Level of (as % of Tier 1 + ALLL) = + $ 34,500

Additional Projected Classified Loans = $ 93,612

Bank Reported Classified Loans = + $ 362,413

Adjusted Projected Classified Loans = $ 456,025

THEREFORE: With 90 % reliability, we infer that actual classified commercial loans should not exceed 132 % of Tier 1 Capital plus ALLL.

PROPORTIONAL SAMPLE EVALUATION WORKSHEET II

Example: This situation is similar to the previous page in data used. However, in this example the sample was taken of a whole commercial loan portfolio consisting of both classified and nonclassified loans. The sample resulted in three loans (all below the cutoff, i.e., the monetary interval) not classified by the bank being classified by examiners, and one internally classified loan being rated "pass" by examiners (denoted by amount in parentheses below). This worksheet reflects the impact of the understatements and the overstatements to the precision factor.

Tier 1 Capital + ALLL: $ 345MM Reliability: 90 % Precision: 10 % Monetary Precision(MP) $ 34.5MM Monetary Interval (MI): $ 15MM

OCC Rating	Borrower	Loan Balance (L)	Sample Exception (SE)	Sample Interval MI/L = SI	Cutoff Loans	Population Exception SExSI = PE	Rank	Precision Adjustment Factor (P)	Precision-adjusted Exception PE x P
		$2,188	$2,188	6.8556		$15,000	1	1.59	$23,850
		$6,007	$2,857	2.4971		$ 7,134	2	1.44	$10,273
		($3,850)	($3,850)	3.8961		($15,000)	1	.10	($ 1,500)
		$ 200	$ 40	75.0000		$ 3,000	3	1.36	$ 4,808
	TOTALS	$5,085				$10,134			$36,703

RESULTS:

Precision-adjusted Exceptions   = $ 36,703

Precision Level of (as % of Tier 1 + ALLL) =   + $ 34,500

        Additional Projected Classified Loans   =   = $ 71,203

Bank Reported Classified Loans   + $ 362,413

        Adjusted Projected Classified Loans   =   = $ 433,616

THEREFORE: With ___90___ % reliability, we infer that actual classified commercial loans should not exceed __126__ % of Tier 1 Capital plus ALLL.

Numerical Sampling

In our example, the objective of performing a numerical sample on override instalment loans is to determine whether they are safely and soundly underwritten and in compliance with any override policy. An exception would be a loan that is not in compliance with policy or not underwritten prudently.

The same evaluation guidance noted in "Proportional Sampling" above is applicable to whether exceptions are found or not.

However, examiners use the following numerical evaluation worksheet to determine the precision-adjusted value of the exceptions.

Numerical Sample Evaluation Worksheet Example

An examiner performed a numerical sample of the instalment loan department to determine compliance with the bank's override underwriting standards. The sample was designed with a 95 percent reliability and 10 percent precision. Two exceptions were found.

Precision (upper limit of the exception rate)	P	10%
Population size	N	1000
Reliability factor	R	3.0
Sample Size	n	30
Sampling interval	I	33
Number of errors	e	2
Sum of the precision adjustment factors = 1.75 + 1.56 =	S	3.31

Error Number	Loan Number	Precision Adjustment Factors
1	12345	1.75
2	54321	1.56
	TOTALS	3.31

$$P' \text{ (revised upper precision limit)} = \frac{33 \times (3.0 + 3.31)}{1000} = .208$$

The revised upper precision limit, .208 or 21 percent, exceeds the sample design upper precision limit of 10 percent. Therefore, the examiner must evaluate the errors and attempt to determine their cause.

If this level of exceptions is unacceptable, the examiner should discuss the results with appropriate bank management and obtain management's commitment to undertake a review and corrective actions.

Probability Statement

A probability statement is a declaration of statistical assurance. Such assurance is a combination of precision and reliability. If an exception rate in a population exceeds some material level (precision), the examiner can state with a certain degree of confidence (i.e., the results have a certain reliability) that the statistical sample will contain a certain number or amount of exceptions. In other words, results of the statistical sample are used to make inferences regarding the entire portfolio (population).

The probability statement only applies to the population from which items were selected statistically. If examiners eliminated a group of items from the population before the sample selection, they cannot evaluate that group of items statistically.

Probability statements cannot be used with nonstatistical judgmental sampling because the results cannot be statistically related to the entire population.

Proportional Sampling

In our example, where the OCC uses proportional sampling to determine additional classified loans in a bank's nonclassified internally rated commercial loan portfolio, a probability statement can inform bank management of the estimated maximum amount of classified loans in that portfolio.

Example with no exceptions: Current internally identified classified commercial loans are 30 percent of Tier 1 capital plus the ALLL. Examiners used an 80 percent reliability level and a 20 percent precision level to review nonclassified commercial loans. Sample results disclosed no exceptions. A probability statement for this sample would be:

> With 80 percent reliability, we infer from our statistical sample that the amount of classified commercial loans will not exceed 50 percent (bank's identified 30 percent plus OCC's precision of 20 percent) of Tier 1 capital plus the ALLL.

Example with exceptions (see the example in the first worksheet): Current internally identified classified commercial loans are 105 percent of Tier 1 capital plus the ALLL. Examiners used a 90 percent reliability level and a 10 percent precision level to examine nonclassified commercial loans. Four exceptions were found. After completing the Proportional Loan Evaluation Worksheet, results disclosed the adjusted precision of those exceptions to be 17 percent. A probability statement for this sample would be:

> With 90 percent reliability, we infer from our statistical sample that the amount of classified commercial loans will not exceed 132 percent of Tier 1 capital plus the ALLL (bank's internally classified 105 percent plus OCC precision of 10 percent plus adjusted precision value of exceptions 17 percent.)

Note: For official purposes in the report of examination and OCC's electronic information systems, the amount and per cent of criticized and classified assets should be derived from the bank's internally identified problem assets adjusted for OCC findings rather than the statistically extrapolated figures. According to the data in the first worksheet, the amount of classified loans to be reflected in the report and in OCC electronic data bases would amount to the more than $362 million identified by the bank plus the $9 million identified by OCC examiners as additional classified loans.

Numerical Sampling

When the OCC uses numerical sampling to determine adherence to bank policies or controls, or compliance with laws and regulations, examiners can use a probability statement to inform bank management of the estimated exception rate in a specified portfolio.

In our example, examiners used numerical sampling to test the accuracy of the instalment loan override underwriting standards.

Example with no exceptions: Examiners set the reliability level at 95 percent and precision level at 10 percent. Thirty loans were reviewed and no exceptions discovered. A probability statement for this sample would be:

> With 95 percent reliability, our statistical sample results indicate that exceptions to the override policy in instalment loans do not exceed 10 percent of the instalment loan portfolio.

Example with two exceptions: Examiners set the reliability level at 95 percent and the precision level at 10 percent. They reviewed 30 loans and discovered two exceptions (see the foregoing "Example of a Numerical Sample Evaluation Worksheet"). A probability statement for this sample would be:

With 95 percent reliability our statistical sample results indicate that exceptions to the override policy in instalment loans do not exceed 21 percent of the instalment loan portfolio.

If the projected level of exceptions is significant or considered unacceptable, examiners should discuss the level with bank management and recommend that management review the situation, determine the extent of the problem, and implement corrective action.

Report of Examination (ROE) Comments

When examiners use statistical sampling and note significant or unacceptable levels of exceptions, they should consider including appropriate language in the applicable ROE comment. The language should include:

- The fact that statistical sampling was used.

- The method of statistical sampling used.

- The number and type of exceptions noted, the underlying root cause of exceptions, and either suggested improvements or management commitments for corrective action.

Examiners should use their own words, rather than statistical language, for report comments. In addition, report comments must be supported by and based on a sufficiently large enough sample size (generally a minimum of 30 items in keeping with accepted statistical industry standards).

Examples of possible ROE comments, including probability statements:

- Proportional sampling

  Currently, bank-identified classified loans in the (describe portfolio reviewed) are (ratio of classified loans to Tier 1 plus the ALLL). During our examination we reviewed a proportional statistical sample of internally rated, nonclassified (identify portfolio reviewed) loans. Our sample disclosed (number or dollar amount of) exceptions indicating that additional unidentified classified loans of ____ percent of Tier 1 capital plus the ALLL may exist. The causes of the sample exceptions were (reason for the exceptions). We recommend that management (suggested corrective action).

Note: For official purposes in the report of examination and OCC's electronic information systems, the amount and percent of criticized and classified assets should be derived from the bank's internally identified problem assets adjusted for OCC findings rather than the statistically extrapolated figures.

Using the first worksheet's data, the amount of classified loans to be reflected in the report and in OCC electronic data bases would amount to the more than $362 million identified by the bank plus the $9 million identified by OCC examiners as additional classified loans.

- Numerical sampling

   During our examination we reviewed a numerical statistical sample of (identify portfolio reviewed) to determine compliance with (describe the specific feature of interest). Our sample disclosed (number) exceptions representing ___ percent of the (identify portfolio). The causes of the sample exceptions were (reason for the exceptions). We recommend that management (suggested corrective action).

1. Determine whether sampling is an efficient and effective tool in evaluating areas of examination interest.

2. Select the sampling method that will achieve the objectives of the supervisory strategy.

3. Use a sample to draw conclusions about the data from which it is taken.

Proportional Sampling

Examiners can use these procedures when dollar amounts are of particular importance and quantifying exceptions or differences in dollars is appropriate, e.g., when sampling the internally rated, nonclassified portions of a bank's loan portfolios.

1. Determine sampling objectives by reviewing the approved supervisory strategy for the bank.

2. Identify and select the population to be reviewed and identify why it is being reviewed.

3. Define the feature of interest for which the identified portfolio is being sampled. For example, in the review of a nonclassified commercial loan portfolio, the feature of interest or exception may be defined as an internally unidentified classified commercial loan.

4. Identify the desired reliability and precision levels for the sample.

   Precision level = _____ %

   Reliability level = _____ %

   Monetary interval = $_____

   $$\frac{(\$ \text{ Tier 1 Capital} + \text{ALLL}) \text{ x precision as a decimal}}{\text{reliability factor (from appendix C based on reliability \%)}}$$

   If reviewing portions of loan portfolios that the bank has not classified, consider the following:

   - Bank loan identification system
     - Bank reviews all loans exceeding $_____

   - Internal identified classification level $_____   %_____

   - Document accuracy of internal identification of past classifications.
     - How do bank ratings compare with OCC classifications?

   - Sample Population $_____
     (Exclude "credit basket" loans and SNC loans if warranted.)

5. Select the sample population. This can be done manually or by using an automated sampling program.

6. Analyze the selected sample items. When analyzing the nonclassified portion of a loan portfolio, consider conducting a minimum file review by screening sampled loans as follows:

    • Is the loans's purpose identified?
    • Is the source of repayment identified and is the loan paying as agreed?
    • Is the loan secured by marketable or liquid collateral?
    • Is the financial statement current and does it support the source or repayment?
    • Does the nature of the business warrant further consideration?

    If the answers suggest that the loan should be classified, conduct a more extensive analysis of the loan using traditional methods.

7. Evaluate the sample results (number of sample exceptions _____)

    • If no exceptions are found, the initial reliability and precision levels are valid.

    • If exceptions are found, determine whether they are a result of inadvertent error or a pattern or practice. Inadvertent exceptions are still exceptions and should not be excluded from sample results. A pattern or practice determination helps with analysis of the sample but does not affect sample results. Determine, based on the type and causes of exceptions, whether additional testing is warranted using the principles of supervision by risk.

    • If sample exceptions exist, adjust the initially selected precision limit to apply sampling results to the entire population. See appendix A for a proportional sample evaluation worksheet that can be prepared manually or using an automated format.

    • If a sample is selected from an entire portfolio (i.e., it includes classified and nonclassified loans), remember to consider both overstatements (loans OCC classified as substandard, doubtful, or loss) and understatements (loans the OCC rates as pass or special mention and the bank classifies as substandard, doubtful, or loss).

8. Document results in working papers and OCC electronic data bases (if significant).

    OCC electronic data base should show:

Bank internally identified classified loans: $ _____

Additional OCC-identified classified loans: $ _____

    Enter total in supervisory data asset statistics
    application $ _____ *

*This figure should not be the statistically extrapolated amount.

9. If warranted, prepare comments for the report of examination, focusing on exceptions and their root causes.

Numerical Sampling

Examiners can use these procedures when sampling loan portfolios or other balance sheet accounts to discover whether a defined feature of interest is present. Such features include compliance with laws or regulations or adherence to a bank's underwriting standards.

1. Determine sampling objectives by reviewing the approved supervisory strategy for the bank.

2. Identify and select the population to be reviewed and why it is being reviewed.

3. Define the feature of interest for which the portfolio is being sampled (e.g., adherence to the bank's underwriting standards for extensions in the instalment loan portfolio.)

4. Identify the reliability and precision levels for the sample.

5. Select the sample population. This can be done manually or by using an automated format.

6. Analyze the selected sample items.

7. Evaluate the sample results (number of sample exceptions_____)

   - If no sample errors are found, the initial reliability and precision levels are valid.

   - If exceptions are found, determine whether they are a result of inadvertent error or a pattern or practice. Inadvertent exceptions are still exceptions and should not be excluded from sample results. A pattern or practice determination helps with analysis of the sample, but does not affect sample results.

   - When sample exceptions exist, adjust the initially selected precision limit to project sampling results for the entire population sampled.

Appendix B's "Numerical Sample Evaluation Worksheet" can be prepared manually to accomplish this. If the sample size is 30 items or more, consider formulating a probability statement.

- Compare the revised precision limit with the original precision limit. If the revised limit exceeds the original one, evaluate the exceptions and attempt to determine their root cause.

- If the exception level is unacceptable, discuss the results with appropriate bank management and obtain a commitment for corrective action.

8. Document results in working papers and in the OCC's electronic data base (if significant).

9. If warranted, prepare comments for the report of examination, focusing on the level of exceptions and their root causes.

PROPORTIONAL SAMPLE EVALUATION WORKSHEET

Tier 1 Capital + ALLL: $ _____   Reliability: _____ %   Precision: _____ %   Monetary Interval (MI): $ _____

OCC Rating	Borrower	Loan Balance (L)	Sample Exception (SE)	Sample Interval MI/L = SI	Cutoff Loans	Population Exception SExSI = PE	Rank	Precision Adjustment Factor (P)	Precision- Adjusted Exception PE x P
TOTALS									

RESULTS: Precision-adjusted Exceptions = _____ $ _____

Precision Level of (as % of Tier 1 + ALLL) = _____ $ _____

Additional Projected Classified Loans = _____ $ _____

Bank Reported Classified Loans = + _____ $ _____

Adjusted Projected Classified Loans = _____ $ _____

THEREFORE: With _____ % reliability, we infer that actual classified loans should not exceed _____ % of Tier 1 capital plus ALLL.

Proportional Sampling Evaluation Worksheet

Instructions

If at least one exception is found, revise the statistical assurance based on sample findings. Raise the precision limits. Do this by completing the following:

OCC Rating:	Enter OCC rating (substandard, doubtful, or loss).
Borrower:	For exceptions, enter borrower's name in Borrower column.
Balance:	Enter loan balance in the Balance (L) column.
Sample Exception:	Enter the dollar amount of the sample exception (SE). This amount may be different from "Balance" when only a portion of the loan is classified. Sample exceptions can be overstatements or understatements. An overstatement is an OCC-classified loan. An understatement is a bank-classified loan that the OCC does not classify. Understatements occur only when the OCC conducts a statistical review of internally classified loans.
Sampling Interval:	Enter the sampling intervals (SI) for each exception. The sampling interval is calculated by dividing the monetary interval by the loan balance (MI/L). The sampling interval is the probability of selecting a loan balance (L) as one of every SI balances of like amount. The sampling interval applies the level of sampling exceptions observed to the population. Sample loan exceptions exceeding the cutoff are always selected; their sampling interval is set at 1.0.
Cutoff Loans:	Enter the dollar amount of loans equal to or exceeding the monetary intervals which are exceptions (CL). Because these loans are selected with certainty, the estimated population exception is the same as the sample exception.
Population Exception:	Obtain the value in this column by multiplying the sample exception (overstatement or understatement loans) by its probability as indicated in the sampling interval column (SE x SI = PE). This statistically projects the value of the sample exception to the population. Record overstatements (or understatements) as appropriate. (NOTE: Loans that are full exceptions will have the monetary interval as its population exception.)

Rank: Rank the population exceptions separately. The exceptions should be ranked in descending order of amounts because of the bias given to larger dollar loan samples in proportional sampling. When exceptions have the same values, rank each separately. Loans exceeding the cutoff are not ranked.

Precision: Enter the adjustment factors for overstatements (appendix C) or understatements (appendix D) based on the reliability of the sample. These factors are used to convert the estimated exceptions in the population into precision-adjusted exceptions. No precision adjustment factor is required for cutoff loans.

Precision   Enter the dollar value of each cutoff loan. For the other
Adjustment   sample exceptions, multiply the population exception by
Exceptions: its precision adjustment factor to yield the precision-adjusted exceptions. The overstatement calculations have increased (and the understatement calculations have decreased) the precision limit based on the sample exceptions so that the same reliability level can be used to evaluate the sample.

               The total of this column and the monetary precision (Tier 1 capital and ALLL x precision percent) represents the potential additional amount of classified loans in the portfolio. This figure is added to the known classified loan totals to estimate the upper limit of classifications.

               A probability statement such as those in this booklet's section "Probability Statement" can then be made using this data.

Additional Evaluation:

     Examiners analyze and evaluate the sample exceptions to determine the root cause and decide whether the sample exceptions are a pattern or practice.

     Consider:
          •   Inexperience of a loan officer.
          •   An exception by type, division, or industry.
          •   Differences by individuals assigning ratings in adhering to internal classification definitions.
          •   Timeliness of bank rating changes.

NUMERICAL SAMPLE EVALUATION WORKSHEET

Sample Design
    Precision   P _____

    Population size   N _____

    Reliability factor (From appendix C, 2.3 for 90%, 3.0 for 95%)   R _____

    Sample size $= \dfrac{R}{P}$ n _____

    Sampling interval $= \dfrac{N}{n}$ I _____

Sample Evaluation
    Number of errors found   e _____

    Sum of the precision adjustment factors   S _____

ERROR NUMBER	LOAN NUMBER	PRECISION ADJUSTMENT FACTOR (From appendix C)
	TOTALS	

Revised upper precision limit $P' = \dfrac{I(R + S)}{N}$

Statistical Sampling Overstatements (OCC classified, bank nonclassified)

Reliability Factors (R)	1.6	2.0	2.3	3.0
Reliability Levels	80%	86%	90%	95%
Rank of Errors[1]	Precision Adjustment Factors (P) For Evaluating Samples at Above Levels			
1	1.39	1.51	1.59	1.75
2	1.28	1.38	1.44	1.56
3	1.24	1.31	1.36	1.46
4	1.21	1.27	1.32	1.40
5	1.19	1.25	1.29	1.36
6	1.17	1.23	1.26	1.33
7	1.16	1.21	1.24	1.31
8	1.15	1.20	1.23	1.29
9	1.14	1.19	1.22	1.28
10	1.14	1.18	1.21	1.26
11	1.13	1.17	1.20	1.25
12	1.13	1.16	1.19	1.24
13	1.12	1.16	1.18	1.23
14	1.12	1.15	1.18	1.22
15-19	1.11	1.15	1.17	1.22
20-24	1.10	1.13	1.15	1.19
25-29	1.09	1.01	1.13	1.17
30-39	1.08	1.00	1.12	1.15
40-49	1.07	1.09	1.10	1.13
50-74	1.06	1.08	1.09	1.12
75-99	1.05	1.07	1.08	1.10
100 and Over	1.04	1.06	1.07	1.09

1   Errors of overstatement should be ranked separately from those of understatement, and within each group the ranking should be from the largest to the smallest amount of error.

Statistical Sampling Understatements (OCC nonclassified, bank classified)

Reliability Factors (R)	1.6	2.0	2.3	3.0
Reliability Levels	80%	86%	90%	95%
Rank of Errors[1]	Precision Adjustment Factors (P) For Evaluating Samples at Above Levels			
1	.22	.14	.10	.05
2	.60	.49	.42	.30
3	.71	.62	.57	.46
4	.76	.69	.64	.54
5	.79	.73	.68	.60
6	.81	.75	.71	.64
7	.83	.77	.74	.67
8	.84	.79	.76	.69
9	.85	.80	.77	.71
10	.86	.81	.78	.73
11	.86	.82	.79	.74
12	.87	.83	.80	.75
13	.87	.84	.81	.76
14	.88	.84	.82	.77
15-19	.88	.85	.83	.78
20-24	.90	.87	85	.81
25-29	.91	.89	.87	.83
30-39	.92	.90	.88	.85
40-49	.93	.91	.90	.87
50-74	.94	.92	.91	.88
75-99	.95	.93	.92	.90
100 and Over	.96	.94	.93	.91

1   The distinction between errors of overstatement and understatement should be based on their effect on the population from which the sample was drawn. If this population is reciprocal to the one of primary interest, errors will have an opposite effect on the population of primary interest.

Adjusted precision level is a recalculated statistical assurance based on the number or monetary amount of tolerable errors noted. If errors are found in a sample, precision must be revised to maintain the original degree of reliability set by the sample plan.

Compliance exception or error is a deviation from established policies, procedures, or practices, i.e., internal control. Examples are noncompliance with loan underwriting standards (such as exceeding approved officer lending limits or failure to obtain required documentation) and violations of laws or regulations (such as incomplete Truth-in-Lending or Truth-in-Savings disclosure statements).

Exception in sampling is an error or deviation in a feature of interest. Exceptions may be monetary (dollar amount) or compliance (nonconformance with policies, procedures, or practices or violations of law or regulation). For example, in a proportional sample of a bank's commercial loan portfolio, an exception is a loan that the bank does not classify internally but the examiners do. In a numerical sample of an instalment loan portfolio, an exception could be a loan that is not in compliance with the bank's underwriting standards or extension, renewal, or override policies (or it could be a loan that is not underwritten in a safe and sound manner).

Feature of interest is the characteristic for which the sample is being taken, e.g., compliance with a regulation or adherence to a bank's policy (such as instalment loan overrides). Features of interest are defined by the objective of the review and commonly are represented as exceptions.

Monetary exception or error causes a dollar amount to be inaccurate. For example, a loan classified by examiners but passed by a bank is a monetary error because it affects the accuracy of the bank's amount of classified assets.

Monetary interval is the dollar measurement used in a proportional sample to select sample items. All items equal to or greater than the dollar amount of the monetary interval will be selected for review.

Nonstatistical or judgmental sampling is the selection of items based on the judgment of an individual. Results of a judgmental sample cannot be used to draw statistically valid inferences about a population.

Numerical statistical sampling is the selection of sample items based on the number of items in a population. No item has a greater probability of being selected than any other and the dollar amount of items is not relevant to sampling objectives (in contrast to proportional statistical sampling). Selection begins from a random starting point and proceeds in a constant measured interval between the selected items.

Poisson distribution expresses the mathematical probabilities that an expected number of exceptions will occur in a selected sample of items from a population in relation to specific confidence intervals (precision and reliability). Appendixes C and D are quick references for parameters associated with the distribution probabilities and precision and reliability levels.

Population is a whole group of related items from which a sample is drawn. For example, all of a bank's internally rated nonclassified notes in its commercial loan portfolio may be the population from which an examiner draws a sample.

Precision, precision limit, or precision level is the amount that sample results can deviate from the most likely results of a review of the entire population and still be acceptable to the examiner. It can be viewed as the OCC's tolerance for the error inherent in not analyzing each item in the population. The OCC allows some imprecision in drawing sample conclusions to avoid analyzing each item in the population. The lower the tolerance for error, the larger the number of items that need to be selected in a sample.

Probability statement is a statement of statistical assurance. Using results of a statistical sample, examiners can draw conclusions about the entire portfolio from which the sample was taken. The probability statement expresses the examiner's degree of confidence that the sample can stand for the entire population.

Proportional statistical sampling is the selection, based on monetary amounts, of items from a population. Larger items have a greater probability of being selected than smaller ones and the dollar amount of items is relevant to sampling objectives (in contrast to numerical statistical sampling). An item's probability of being selected is proportional to its monetary amount relative to an established monetary interval.

Reliability or reliability level is the probability that the value of the feature of interest in the sample is representative of the entire population, i.e., within the desired precision level. Reliability is a reflection of the degree of confidence an examiner has in the sample results and how much risk of imprecision she or he is willing to accept.

Reliability factor is a mathematically calculated approximation of the probability of finding at least one exception in a sample of selected items at a given reliability level and error rate. Reliability factors are used to determine sample sizes and precision adjustment factors. They are common references for audit sampling purposes. See appendixes C and D.

Sample, sample items or sample population is the group of items selected, using a sampling method, from a larger general population.

Sample interval is the constant measured interval between items selected for a sample. This interval can be every nth item, e.g., every 10th item. Intervals can also be a set distance or position between items or the terminal digits of population items.

Sample plan is the process of setting objectives for the sample, selecting the population to be sampled, designing and selecting the sample, and evaluating and interpreting sample results.

Sampling risk is the risk that the sample is not representative of the entire population. Sampling risk is determined by a formula — 1 minus the reliability level as a decimal. For example, with 90 percent reliability, the sampling risk is 10 percent (1 - .90 = .10). This means that 10 percent of the time, or one time in ten, the results of the sample may not be indicative of the entire portfolio.

Statistical assurance, a product of precision and reliability, is the measure of reliance an examiner places on inferences drawn using the sample. It is commonly expressed in a probability statement.

Statistical or sample projection uses probability theory to apply sample results to the entire population sampled and depends on a random selection process. To understand probability theory, examiners must understand reliability and precision, as well as their interrelationship.